THE ABC's OF LIVING WITH A DACHSHUND

BY

Judith Keim and Peter Keim

Wild Quail Publishing

No part of *The ABC's of Living With A Dachshund* may be reproduced or transmitted in any form or by any electronic or mechanical means, including information storage and retrieval systems, without permission in writing from the author, except by a reviewer who may quote brief passages in a review. This book may not be resold or uploaded for distribution to others. For permissions contact the author directly via electronic mail:

wildquail.pub@gmail.com

www.judithkeim.com

Wild Quail Publishing
PO Box 171332
Boise, ID 83717-1332

ISBN 978-1-954325-29-6
Copyright ©2021 Judith Keim
All rights reserved

Dedication

To Tio, Noodle, Willy, Trinka, Winston, and Wally

For all the joys you've given us.

PROLOGUE

New owners and repeat owners of Dachshunds are often dazzled, puzzled, and outmaneuvered by their darling little wieners. Helplessly, they watch their lives being overtaken with a yip here and a yap there.

Don't speak "Dachshundese"?

It's not quite as easy as learning *our* ABC's but any respectable Dachshund (or many other dogs) would admit that the following definitions give a broader understanding of the world s/he dominates.

Enjoy the journey! And give that jaunty, marvelous pet a hug and a kiss!

YIP! YAP! GOT IT?

A DACHSHUND DICTIONARY
For Soon-to-be Enlightened Dog Owners

ACCELERATE – v. To induce forward motion by increasingly rapid movement of short, crooked legs. The process of acceleration is frequently characterized by differential rates when the forward half of the elongated body is overrun by the rear half.

Especially prone to happen when rounding corners, causing spinouts, rollovers and other similar acrobatic maneuvers. (See **JACKKNIFE**).

AGREEABLE – Adj. The condition or state of mind of a Dachshund when all things are going his way and he is in complete control. How the dog feels when no further comforts can be bestowed.

ANYTHING – n. All that is within view that could be of possible interest and/or comfort. Interest in **ANYTHING** is expressed by an unwavering stare and a fixed, unmoving stance at attention, ears perked. If that approach fails, the Dachshund is likely to begin barking repeatedly to let you know the time has come to "cut the crap" and hand it (**ANYTHING**) over.

ATTACK – v. Rapid **ACCELERATION** in the direction of **ANYTHING** that is out of reach, generally with a spirit of territorial **DEFENSE**. Behavior is altered in one of two ways as the dog comes closer to the object. The barking becomes more shrill (See **YIP, YAP**) or the dog rolls over for a **TUMMY RUB**.

BABY – n. What a Dachshund acts like more often than not.
v. How a Dachshund would like to be treated.

BALL – n. A round object, usually of rubber, that causes intense excitement on the part of one's owner, typically expressed with a toss and a command to "Get the ball!" The Dachshund's interest remains high throughout the process, waiting to see how long it will take the owner to become discouraged by his unwillingness to follow the command (See **OBEDIENCE**). Great **PLEASURE** is shown by the dog upon seeing the owner retrieve the **BALL** and throw it again. (See **FETCH**). Eventually the owner is trained.

BEG – v. To act in a manner indicative of desire to

receive a treat or other morsel of **FOOD** or attention. Can be accompanied by a low whine, soft **YIPS,** or even a brief **HOWL.**

BONE – n. The skeletal remains of a steak or roast that finds its way into the dog's possession after much jumping, **LEAPING**, and turning in circles while barking excitedly. (See **ANYTHING**). Alternately, a hard plastic object resembling skeletal remains purchased by the owner in a feeble attempt to persuade the dog that the real thing will not be forthcoming; frequently found lying in a corner gathering dust.

BOWL – n. An object designed to hold a dog's dinner, usually located on the **KITCHEN** floor adjacent to the water dish. Makes its own unique sound when lifted from the floor to the counter, causing intense interest in the Dachshund, accompanied by **LEAPING** off the floor, circling about, **YIPS, YAPS,** and excess salivation. (See **ANYTHING, LEAP, YIP, YAP**). A **BOWL** is best liked when filled with **ANYTHING** other than dog food. However, Dachshunds have never been known to turn down **FOOD** of any kind.

CAN OPENER – n. A device used to make **FOOD** accessible for placement in a **BOWL**. Makes a characteristic sound that, when heard in conjunction with the bowl's arrival on the counter, intensifies the Dachshund's **LEAPING**, circling about, and salivation (See **BOWL**).

CAT – n. A four-legged beast that delights in teasing Dachshunds by ignoring, until the last possible moment, the sounds of **ATTACK** from the onrushing dog. (See **ATTACK**). This behavior causes the frenzied Dachshund to chase in circles long after the **CAT** has disappeared.

COLLAR –n. A medieval torture device used to encircle a Dachshund's neck for the purpose of controlling the dog's **DIRECTION** when attached to a **LEASH**. Also used to restrain the dog from **ATTACKING ANYTHING**. May serve a decorative purpose when used to hold a red ribbon at the holiday season. In summer collars are often accompanied by a white band rumored to ward off insects.

COOKIE – n. Any small, edible biscuit or similar treat received in recognition for accomplishing an important activity such as going outdoors, looking cute, or maintaining control of one's "master" by excessive **NAGGING**.

COME – v. A word that does not exist in any self-respecting Dachshund's vocabulary. (See **SIT, STAY, LIE DOWN, QUIET, ROLL OVER**).

CRATE – n. A device used by an owner to restrict the Dachshund from **SALLYING FORTH** within the house or while riding in the car. Can induce the dog to whine and **HOWL** incessantly if not trained to tolerate the crate.

DAWDLE – v. To move at one's own pre-programmed pace, totally **IGNORING** an owner's desire. Dawdling provides another method of asserting control over an owner.

DEFENSE – n. The principal purpose of every journey taken outside of the house (see **SALLY FORTH**), especially if another dog has been in the neighborhood within the last day or two. The volume and pace of barking to announce **DEFENSE** varies inversely with the amount of time that has elapsed since the interloping dog was last in the vicinity.

DEFIANT – adj. A demeanor that results in many repetitions of activities that annoy the owner, such as getting into the garbage, digging in the garden, **LEAPING** onto furniture and doing exactly as the Dachshund pleases. (See **DEFIANT, FORAGE, LEAP**)

DIRECTION – n. An order by the owner, something no real Dachshund ever pays any attention to. When outdoors on **DEFENSE**, varies rapidly when attacking **SQUIRRELS**, chipmunks, and **CATS** with the intent of trying to scare same. (See **ATTACK, DEFENSE**).

EARNEST – adj. A Dachshund's attitude upon initiating an **ATTACK**. The degree of earnestness varies inversely with the distance from the object under attack unless the object is edible. If said object is a dog larger than the Dachshund, the earnest attitude varies inversely with the square of the distance.

EARS – n. Appendages attached to the Dachshund's head, useful for flapping rapidly when shaking its head. The principal purpose of ears, however, is to be scratched. (See **SCRITCH**).

EFFUSIVE – adj. The kind of reception an owner can expect after a visit to the grocery store just before dinnertime. Varies directly with the number of bags carried in and placed on the counter.

FELINE – adj. Of or pertaining to a **CAT**. A trait disliked by most Dachshunds.

FETCH – v. An activity usually performed by a stubborn dog's owner after repeated requests to the Dachshund to "Get the ball!". (See **BALL**).

FOOD – n. The staff of life. Takes many forms, the lowest of which comes in a can labeled "Dog Food." Something of which there is never enough.

FORAGE – v. An activity undertaken by Dachshund when not on **DEFENSE**. The principal objective of foraging is the acquisition of **FOOD**. Primary sources are children's plates, the cupboard under the **KITCHEN** sink, and the neighbor's trash. (See **GARBAGE**).

GAIT – n. The style with which a Dachshund walks, trots, or runs on short, crooked legs. When trotting quickly or running, the legs form a blur. Varies with mood or situation. (See **HANG DOG**).

GARBAGE – n. The name given by an owner to some of the most interesting kinds of **FOOD** accessible when **FORAGING**. Generally found under the sink in the **KITCHEN** or along the curb outside in large plastic sacks. Dachshunds are **DEFIANT** in their commitment to gaining access to garbage. (See **DEFIANT**).

GASTRONOMY – n. Something with which Dachshunds do not concern themselves since they are omnivorous. (See **GARBAGE**).

GIRTH – n. The circumference of a dog taken at the roundest section of the body. Generally increases with age, making Dachshunds little different from their owners. Varies directly with success at **FORAGING**.

GROOMING – v. An event generally enjoyed by long-hair Dachshunds until the groomer undertakes certain procedures such as nail trimming or cleaning teeth. (See **TOOTHBRUSH)**

HANG DOG – adj. Of or pertaining to a Dachshund's facial expression when caught 'red-pawed' **FORAGING** in the **GARBAGE**. Characterized by drooping ears and a slinking **GAIT** in the direction away from its owner.

HAPPY – adj. Descriptive of the demeanor of a Dachshund who has been recently fed, is lying on a blanket in front of a fire, and is having its ears scritched. (See **AGREEABLE**).

HEARTBROKEN – adj. What a Dachshund would have you believe he is when you leave without him. Characterized by drooping ears, frequent attempts to get in the car and, upon the owner's actual departure, immediate **ACCELERATION** toward the most comfortable chair in the house. A demeanor brought on by the sight of suitcases being packed. (See **HOWL**)

HOG – v. What a Dachshund does after jumping onto a chair or the couch, especially if the owner is currently sitting on said chair or couch.

HOWL – v. A noise made by a Dachshund whenever the owner leaves the dog at home while running errands or otherwise seeking relief from the dog's demands. (See **QUIET**)

INTELLIGENT – adj. How a Dachshund's owner describes him to the owners of other dogs but foresworn when attempting to persuade the Dachshund to do something. (See **COME, FETCH, STAY, LIE DOWN, SIT, ROLL OVER, BALL, DAWDLE, IGNORE, OATH**).

IMPORTANCE – n. A sense or feeling common to Dachshunds that is consistent with their concept of their place in the world. (See **PREDESTINATION**).

IRRESISTIBLE – adj. Descriptive of puppies in general and of grown dogs upon being treated in the manner that makes them most **AGREEABLE**. (See **BABY**).

JACKKNIFE – v. To round a corner so fast that the rear end loses control and crashes into a wall or door jamb, upending the rest of the body. (See **ACCELERATE**).

JAUNDICED – adj. Of or pertaining to the eye given its owner by Dachshund when offered less-than-desirable food or when mention is made of a trip to the **VET**.

JURISDICTION – n. Wherever a Dachshund is at any time. (See **KINGDOM**).

KENNEL – n. A six-letter, blasphemous word never to be uttered in a Dachshund's presence. A place where a Dachshund goes if the neighbors refuse to participate in its care because of previous **FORAGING** or **STUBBORN** behavior.

KINGDOM – n. Wherever a Dachshund is at any time. (See **JURISDICTION**).

KITCHEN – n. The room in the house where **FORAGING** can be most successful. The opportune location to obtain a variety of tidbits by being **UNDERFOOT** and performing other tricks. (See **ANYTHING**).

KITTEN – n. A small version of **CAT**, one which offers a Dachshund in **ATTACK** a greater chance of success.

LEAP – v. The act of propelling oneself upward in enthusiasm in anticipation of **FOOD** or in expectation of landing on a piece of furniture.

LEASH – n. Another medieval torture device designed to restrain Dachshunds from free activities. Under the right circumstances, Dachshund will feign enthusiasm upon seeing a leash and hearing the term "**WALK**."

MALINGER – v. What a Dachshund attempts to do upon arrival at the **VET'S** office. Frequently accompanied by a **HANG-DOG** expression. Characterized by attempts to **ACCELERATE** in any direction away from the door to the office. (See **VET**.)

MASTER – n. A word rejected by any respectable Dachshund. The mistaken impression a dog's owner has of himself.

MEAL - n. The highlight of a Dachshund's day; an event that can occur at any time. If this event does not occur with sufficient frequency, it causes increased efforts on the Dachshund's part to **NAG** and, if further ignored, will initiate indiscriminate **FORAGING**.

NAG – v. To sit or stand in view of the owner with imploring eyes and unwavering stare. If ignored for any length of time, low moans or other sounds of pain and anguish occur. Upon making eye contact with the owner, tail wagging and salivation begin simultaneously. Success is achieved when the Dachshund receives his **MEAL** before the owner does.

NAP – n. A Dachshund's second favorite event, particularly in a patch of sunshine or on a couch within easy reach of the owner, allowing napping and ear scrItching simultaneously. (See **SCRITCH**).

NOSE – n. The elongated portion of a Dachshund's head, having a black, cold tip, useful in foraging and preparing **ATTACKS**. An effective tool in abruptly awakening one's owner to secure a warm spot, enabling the Dachshund to begin nestling. (See **HOG**).

NOSEPRINT – n. What results on the inside of an owner's car windows after taking the Dachshund for a

RIDE. Also found on any **WINDOW** or door in the house, especially those adjacent to a piece of furniture from which the Dachshund can observe his **KINGDOM** at a higher level. Noseprints most often appear on windows that have just been washed.

OATH – n. The word or words an owner utters upon observing a Dachshund's **DAWDLING** or the results of its mischievous behavior. The final action taken by an owner when attempting to counter a Dachshund's **STUBBORNNESS**.

OBEDIENCE – n. Another concept unheard of to Dachshunds. (See **COME, FETCH, ROLL OVER, SIT, STAY, IGNORE, OATH**).

OBLIVIOUS – adj. The state of mind of a Dachshund in respect to anything other than the focus of its attention. (see **ATTACK, FORAGE, IGNORE**).

OPTIMIST – n. What a Dachshund becomes when initiating an **ATTACK**; the spirit of optimism varies directly with the age and inversely with the physical condition of the object under attack.

OUT – n. A place where a Dachshund does not want to go when it is snowing or raining or cold. When these conditions become known to the dog, it will attempt to **ACCELERATE** away from the door and hide under a **TABLE**.

PAPER – n. A substance placed on the floor by an owner of a young Dachshund; used for ripping, tearing, chewing, and scattering about. Once such activity has taken place, the Dachshund is then able to create another mess in the middle of a carpet. Most effective when the carpet is new. (See **PUDDLE**)

PARDON – v. An action undertaken by a disappointed Dachshund once the owner has placed a **MEAL** in the **BOWL** and the ears have been **SCRITCHED**.

PAT – n. A poor substitute for a **SCRITCH** or a hug.

PLEASURE – n. The result of having ears scritched, being fed, or taking over an owner's warm spot. (See **AGREEABLE**).

PREDESTINATION – n. The certainty a Dachshund feels when considering its place in the world. An understanding that a Dachshund was meant to rule. (See **KINGDOM**).

PUDDLE – n. The result when a young Dachshund is not put outside immediately after a **NAP**; typically found on that portion of the **KITCHEN** floor not covered by **PAPER**.

QUICK – adj. Descriptive of a Dachshund's ability to see an opportunity, especially for foraging. Of or pertaining to the **GAIT** of a Dachshund when under **ATTACK** by a larger dog.

QUIET – adj. A behavior the Dachshund refuses to adhere to when asked. The request for this behavior is especially ineffective when accompanied by an attempt on the owner's part to reason with the dog.

RABIES SHOT – n. Why one goes to the **VET**. An event looked upon by the Dachshund with as much anticipation as the owner feels about going to the dentist. (See **VET**)

RANKLE – v. What a Dachshund's mischievous activities do to an owner, causing an outbreak of angry words. (See **OATH**).

RATION – v. Another concept foreign to Dachshunds. To a Dachshund, anything worth having, is worth having in large quantities. (See **FOOD, MEAL**).

RIDE – n. A word that causes great interest when mentioned to the Dachshund. The prospect of a ride inspires the dog to **ACCELERATE** in the direction of the car and to **LEAP** into the driver's seat, where it stubbornly remains.

ROLL OVER – v. Yet another command from an owner usually **IGNORED** by a Dachshund. An action instituted voluntarily by a Dachshund when there is the slightest hint that a **TUMMY RUB** may be in the offing.

SALLY FORTH – v. To venture out on any mission with the intent of **FORAGING**, defending one's turf, finding a patch of sun to lie in, or digging in the garden. Carried out in a jaunty manner with a great deal of noise. (See **QUIET, YIP, YAP, IGNORE, OATH**).

SCRITCH – n. The act of simultaneously rubbing and scratching a Dachshund's ears. Done in a manner that produces a variety of noises expressing **PLEASURE**. (See **AGREEABLE**).

SIT – v. A command generally **IGNORED** by a Dachshund, unless it decides to go no further, despite implorings from the owner to stop dawdling and come along. (See **DAWDLE**).

SNARL – v. What a Dachshund will likely do when confronted by a larger and aggressive dog while out on a walk, or, alternatively, with regret, whenever the owner tries to remove yet-uneaten **FOOD** or unauthorized snacks from the dog.

SQUIRREL – n. The sworn enemy, the object of many **ATTACKS**, few of which are in the right direction. A skilled adversary who races up the nearest tree just high enough to be viewed easily, causing the Dachshund to **LEAP** and bark at the tree long after the squirrel has left the neighborhood.

STAY – v. A command that a Dachshund cannot believe is directed toward him, as all Dachshunds believe they have the right to participate in the activities of their choice. (See **IGNORE**).

STUBBORN – adj. Expressed by a persistent attitude when a Dachshund focuses its attention on a particular idea to the exclusion of all else, notwithstanding the approach of danger, the owner, or any command. (See **IGNORE, OBLIVIOUS**). An offer of **FOOD** has been known to break a stubborn attitude.

TABLE – n. A piece of furniture under which a Dachshund expresses its most fervent **OPTIMISM**. The object under which a Dachshund hides when an owner is trying to persuade him about the necessity of going outside on a cold, snowy night. (See **OUT**).

THIN – adj. A physical attribute that is never considered by a Dachshund. An impediment to foraging.

TOOTHBRUSH – n. A device used by an owner or the groomer to clean the Dachshund's teeth. Generally not liked by the dog, who may resist efforts at its use by clamping mouth shut and turning its head away. (See **GROOMING**).

TUMMY RUB – n. The circular or linear stroking of a Dachshund's chest and/or stomach while the dog is on its back. One of the methods of making a Dachshund happy. (See **AGREEABLE**).

UBIQUITOUS – adj. The location of a Dachshund when small children are eating and spilling **FOOD** within its range. Characterized by darting and dashing, stopping only long enough to finish one tidbit and **FORAGE** for another.

UNDERFOOT – adj. A Dachshund's spot in the kitchen whenever **FOOD** is being prepared. Accompanied by much scurrying and jockeying to obtain tidbits that may fall carelessly (or be dropped deliberately) to the floor. Accompanied by an anticipatory expression, salivation, occasional **YIPS**, whines and other forms of **NAGGING**.

UNIVERSE – n. That which a Dachshund controls. (See

JURISDICITON, KINGDOM).

UNREQUITED – adj. A condition unheard of by Dachshunds who, having determined those worthy of proper love and affection, ensure the reciprocity of their affection by wiggling, waggling and licking with abandon.

VEHEMENT – adj. The general demeanor of a Dachshund when indicating a way in which an owner can bring about a state of happiness. (See **AGREEABLE**).

VELOCITY – adj. The speed at which a Dachshund **ACCELERATES**. Increased when running toward **FOOD** or away from a dog larger than itself. The velocity of a Dachshund varies greatly during **ATTACK**. (See **CAT, KITTEN**).

VERSATILE – adj. Descriptive of a Dachshund's actions when trying to obtain a desired object or action. (See **ANYTHING**).

VICTIM – n. The feeling an owner sometimes has when trying to deal with a Dachshund. (See **ANYTHING, HOG, IGNORE, OATH**).

VET – n. a word best not mentioned in the presence of

the Dachshund. Generally produces a **HANG-DOG** look and many efforts to avoid being taken to and put into the car. Also, a place where, upon being discharged, anxiety to leave is illustrated by lunges for the exit door or anywhere outside of the office.

WAG – n. The beginning of a **WIGGLE**. Used to express encouragement to an owner, indicating it is time to bring about a state of **AGREEABLENESS** to the Dachshund.

WALK – n. A word that induces great excitement on the part of a Dachshund, unless it is cold, snowy, or rainy.

WIGGLE – n. The end result of many **WAGS**. An effective means of gaining **ANYTHING** desired, especially when accompanied by licks and **LEAPS**. A true wiggle involves movement from the tip of the dog's nose to the tip of his tail.

WINDOW – n. Something through which a Dachshund maintains a vigil over his domain. (See **JURISDICTION, KINGDOM, NOSEPRINT**).

XMAS – adj. The kind of day an owner has when his Dachshund is **AGREEABLE**, the owner has been welcomed, and nothing else can be done to improve the atmosphere.

YAP – n. A high-pitched bark signaling great anxiety on the part of the Dachshund. Usually presented upon seeing a **CAT** or another object of **ATTACK**, or upon becoming uncertain about whether a comfort is about to be bestowed. (see **ANYTHING**). A lesser degree of **YIP**.

YARD – n. The area which a Dachshund is dedicated to guarding when the owner is at home. Often considered to be an unimportant boundary when the owner is away, especially if the Dachshund is lying in a patch of sun in a neighbor's yard.

YIP – n. A higher pitched **YAP**. (See **YAP**).

ZEAL – adj. The way in which a Dachshund undertakes anything. (See **ATTACK, FORAGE**).

ZILCH – n. The score an owner achieves when trying to outwit a Dachshund. (See **OATH**).

ZZZZZ's – n. The sound a Dachshund makes when stretched out dozing. Increased if said dog is lying down in front of a fireplace or in a patch of sun, having its ears **SCRITCHED**.

About the Authors

Judith Keim and Peter Keim live in Idaho with their two latest dachshunds, **Winston and Wally**. Like many young couples, their first "child" was a dog, in particular, a dachshund. **Tio** began their life-long journey with dachshunds, eventually joining their two sons and continuing to fill their lives after their boys became independent.

Judith, a writer of women's fiction, enjoyed her childhood and young-adult years in Elmira, New York. While growing up, she was drawn to the idea of writing stories from a young age. Books were always present, being read, ready to go back to the library, or about to be discovered. All in her family shared information from the books in general conversation, giving them a wealth of knowledge and vivid imaginations.

A hybrid author who both has a publisher and self-publishes, Ms. Keim writes heart-warming novels about women who face unexpected challenges, meet them with strength, and find love and happiness along the way. Her best-selling books are based, in part, on many of the places she's lived or visited and on the interesting people she's met, creating believable characters and realistic settings her many loyal readers love. Ms. Keim loves to hear from her readers and appreciates their enthusiasm for her stories.

To sign up for her newsletter, go here: http://eepurl.com/bZoICX

Her website: **http://www.judithkeim.com/**

BOOKS BY JUDITH KEIM

THE HARTWELL WOMEN SERIES:
- The Talking Tree – 1
- Sweet Talk – 2
- Straight Talk – 3
- Baby Talk – 4
- The Hartwell Women – Boxed Set

THE BEACH HOUSE HOTEL SERIES:
- Breakfast at The Beach House Hotel – 1
- Lunch at The Beach House Hotel – 2
- Dinner at The Beach House Hotel – 3
- Christmas at The Beach House Hotel – 4
- Margaritas at The Beach House Hotel – 5
- Dessert at The Beach House Hotel – 6 (2022)

THE FAT FRIDAYS GROUP:
- Fat Fridays – 1
- Sassy Saturdays – 2
- Secret Sundays – 3

SALTY KEY INN BOOKS:
- Finding Me – 1
- Finding My Way – 2
- Finding Love – 3
- Finding Family – 4

SEASHELL COTTAGE BOOKS:
- A Christmas Star
- Change of Heart
- A Summer of Surprises

A Road Trip to Remember
The Beach Babes – (2022)

CHANDLER HILL INN BOOKS:
Going Home – 1
Coming Home – 2
Home at Last – 3

DESERT SAGE INN BOOKS:
The Desert Flowers – Rose – 1
The Desert Flowers – Lily – 2 (Oct. 2021)
The Desert Flowers – Willow – 3 (2022)
The Desert Flowers – Mistletoe & Holly – 4 (2022)

Winning BIG – a little love story for all ages

The ABC's of Living With A Dachshund

For more information: http://amzn.to/2jamIaF

PRAISE FOR JUDITH KEIM'S NOVELS

THE BEACH HOUSE HOTEL SERIES

"*Love the characters in this series. This series was my first introduction to Judith Keim. She is now one of my favorites. Looking forward to reading more of her books.*"
BREAKFAST AT THE BEACH HOUSE HOTEL *is an easy, delightful read that offers romance, family relationships, and strong women learning to be stronger. Real life situations filter through the pages. Enjoy!*"
LUNCH AT THE BEACH HOUSE HOTEL – "*This series is such a joy to read. You feel you are actually living with them. Can't wait to read the latest one.*"
DINNER AT THE BEACH HOUSE HOTEL – "*A Terrific Read! As usual, Judith Keim did it again. Enjoyed immensely. Continue writing such pleasantly reading books for all of us readers.*"
CHRISTMAS AT THE BEACH HOUSE HOTEL – "*Not Just Another Christmas Novel. This is book number four in the series and my introduction to Judith Keim's writing. I wasn't disappointed. The characters are dimensional and engaging. The plot is well crafted and advances at a pleasing pace. The Florida location is interesting and warming. It was a delight to read a romance novel with mature female protagonists. Ann and Rhoda have life experiences that enrich the story. It's a clever book about friends and extended family. Buy copies for your book group pals and enjoy this seasonal read.*"
MARGARITAS AT THE BEACH HOIUSE HOTEL – "*What a wonderful series. I absolutely loved this book and can't wait for the next book to come out. There was even suspense in it. Thanks Judith for the great stories.*"

"Overall, Margaritas at the Beach House Hotel is another wonderful addition to the series. Judith Keim takes the reader on a journey told through the voices of these amazing characters we have all come to love through the years! I truly cannot stress enough how good this book is, and I hope you enjoy it as much as I have!"

THE HARTWELL WOMEN SERIES – Books 1 – 4

"This was an EXCELLENT series. When I discovered Judith Keim, I read all of her books back to back. I thoroughly enjoyed the women Keim has written about. They are believable and you want to just jump into their lives and be their friends! I can't wait for any upcoming books!"

"I fell into Judith Keim's Hartwell Women series and have read & enjoyed all of her books in every series. Each centers around a strong & interesting woman character and their family interaction. Good reads that leave you wanting more."

THE FAT FRIDAYS GROUP – Books 1 – 3

"Excellent story line for each character, and an insightful representation of situations which deal with some of the contemporary issues women are faced with today."

"I love this author's books. Her characters and their lives are realistic. The power of women's friendships is a common and beautiful theme that is threaded throughout this story."

THE SALTY KEY INN SERIES

<u>FINDING ME</u> – "I thoroughly enjoyed the first book in this series and cannot wait for the others! The characters are endearing with the same struggles we all encounter. The setting makes me feel like I am a guest at The Salty Key Inn...relaxed, happy & light-hearted! The men are yummy and the women strong. You can't get better than that! Happy Reading!"

<u>FINDING MY WAY</u> - *"Loved the family dynamics as well as uncertain emotions of dating and falling in love. Appreciated the morals and strength of parenting throughout. Just couldn't put this book down."*

<u>FINDING LOVE</u> – *"I waited for this book because the first two was such good reads. This one didn't disappoint…. Judith Keim always puts substance into her books. This book was no different, I learned about PTSD, accepting oneself, there is always going to be problems but stick it out and make it work. Just the way life is. In some ways a lot like my life. Judith is right, it needs another book and I will definitely be reading it. Hope you choose to read this series, you will get so much out of it."*

<u>FINDING FAMILY</u> – *"Completing this series is like eating the last chip. Love Judith's writing, and her female characters are always smart, strong, vulnerable to life and love experiences."*

"This was a refreshing book. Bringing the heart and soul of the family to us."

CHANDLER HILL INN SERIES

<u>GOING HOME</u> – *"I absolutely could not put this book down. Started at night and read late into the middle of the night. As a child of the '60s, the Vietnam war was front and center so this resonated with me. All the characters in the book were so well developed that the reader felt like they were friends of the family."*

"I was completely immersed in this book, with the beautiful descriptive writing, and the authors' way of bringing her characters to life. I felt like I was right inside her story."

<u>COMING HOME</u> – *"Coming Home is a winner. The characters are well-developed, nuanced and likable. Enjoyed the vineyard setting, learning about wine growing and seeing the challenges Cami faces in running and growing a business. I look forward to the next book in this series!"*

"Coming Home was such a wonderful story. The author has such a gift for getting the reader right to the heart of things."

HOME AT LAST – "In this wonderful conclusion, to a heartfelt and emotional trilogy set in Oregon's stunning wine country, Judith Keim has tied up the Chandler Hill series with the perfect bow."

"Overall, this is truly a wonderful addition to the Chandler Hill Inn series. Judith Keim definitely knows how to perfectly weave together a beautiful and heartfelt story."

"The storyline has some beautiful scenes along with family drama. Judith Keim has created characters with interactions that are believable and some of the subjects the story deals with are poignant."

SEASHELL COTTAGE BOOKS

A CHRISTMAS STAR – "Love, laughter, sadness, great food, and hope for the future, all in one book. It doesn't get any better than this stunning read."

"A Christmas Star is a heartwarming Christmas story featuring endearing characters. So many Christmas books are set in snowbound places...it was a nice change to read a Christmas story that takes place on a warm sandy beach!" Susan Peterson

CHANGE OF HEART – "CHANGE OF HEART is the summer read we've all been waiting for. Judith Keim is a master at creating fascinating characters that are simply irresistible. Her stories leave you with a big smile on your face and a heart bursting with love."
~Kellie Coates Gilbert, author of the popular Sun Valley Series

A SUMMER OF SURPRISES – "The story is filled with a roller coaster of emotions and self-discovery. Finding love again and rebuilding family relationships."

"Ms. Keim uses this book as an amazing platform to show that with hard emotional work, belief in yourself and love, the scars of abuse can be conquered. It in no way preaches, it's a lovely story with a happy ending."

"The character development was excellent. I felt I knew these people my whole life. The story development was very well thought out I was drawn [in] from the beginning."

DESERT SAGE INN BOOKS

<u>THE DESERT FLOWERS – ROSE</u> – "*The Desert Flowers - Rose, is the first book in the new series by Judith Keim. I always look forward to new books by Judith Keim, and this one is definitely a wonderful way to begin The Desert Sage Inn Series!*"

"In this first of a series, we see each woman come into her own and view new beginnings even as they must take this tearful journey as they slowly lose a dear friend. This is a very well written book with well-developed and likable main characters. It was interesting and enlightening as the first portion of this saga unfolded. I very much enjoyed this book and I do recommend it"

"Judith Keim is one of those authors that you can always depend on to give you a great story with fantastic characters. I'm excited to know that she is writing a new series and after reading book 1 in the series, I can't wait to read the rest of the books."!

CHILDREN'S BOOKS BY J. S. KEIM

THE HIDDEN MOON SERIES:
    The Hidden Moon – 1
    Return to the Hidden Moon – 2
    Trouble on the Hidden Moon – 3)

Kermit Greene's World

For more information: http://amzn.to/2qlqKMI

PRAISE FOR J. S. KEIM'S BOOKS

THE HIDDEN MOON

"The Hidden Moon is a wonderful fantasy escape for middle grades. As Jack, Collin and Danny come to know the people of Anron and are called to help them regain their freedom. The book is filled with shape-shifters, flying dragons and fun. I bought a copy for my grandson for Christmas and am hoping for more from this author."
Amazon Review

"My granddaughter, age 9, loved this book, so it's not a book you should limit to just middle-grade kids. J. S. Keim has a great imagination that appeals to kids and she adds to that wonderful powers of description. This is a must read for both boys and girls and will definitely appeal to both. A great gift idea for hooking kids on reading and for inspiring their imaginations. They will love it!!!"
Amazon Review

"A fun story filled with adventure and suspense. I liked that the author took time to really plan out the story and the characters, and you don't know what might happen next." Amazon Review

"*Fun read, enjoyable for both adult and child; its high adventure for young space jockies. Want to encourage your kids to read more? This is a good book for that purpose.*" Amazon Review

RETURN TO THE HIDDEN MOON

"*There are heroes and villains . . . and bad-guy problems. But the kids get to sort it all out. Some of the "bad-guys" turn around, become "good-guys." That's a positive message for youngsters who read these books, and exactly what should be expected of an adventure story for young boys and girls.*" Amazon Review

"*The magic that carries the two brothers and their friend off to another planet is every young person's dream. And all the creatures they encounter, who are mostly good, are described in such vivid detail. I could see them in my own imaginations. Of course, there are the bad guys, but this is what keeps the book exciting.*" Amazon Review

KERMIT GREENE'S WORLD

"*As I was reading this delightful book, I kept thinking how much I wished I'd had this when I was teaching. My gifted students loved doing a bird-eye and bug-eye sketch of the same item and this would have been great to read to go along with that. Also, as a former teacher, I loved how math was interwoven in the story during a pivotal point in the plot.*

Great book for all kids and a fabulous addition to any teacher's classroom set of books." Amazon Review

"*What a great book for children to transition into becoming readers. This is exciting, fun to read and delights the imagination!*" Amazon Review

Made in the USA
Monee, IL
28 August 2021